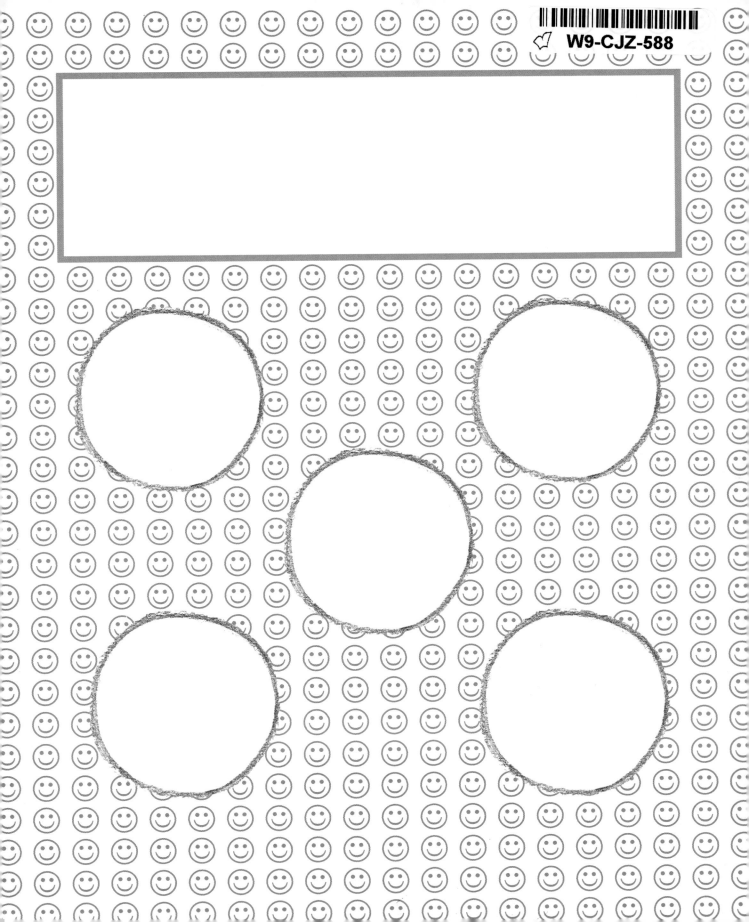

Josh's Smiley Faces

A STORY ABOUT
ANGER

Published by
MAGINATION PRESS
An Educational Publishing Foundation Book
American Psychological Association
750 First Street, NE
Washington, DC 20002

For more information about our books, including a complete catalog, please write to us, call 1-800-374-2721, or visit our website at www.maginationpress.com.

Editor: Darcie Conner Johnston
Art Director: Susan K. White
The text type is Sabon.
Printed by Phoenix Color, Rockaway, New Jersey

Library of Congress Cataloging-in-Publication Data

Ditta-Donahue, Gina.
     Josh's smiley faces : a story about anger / written by Gina Ditta-Donahue ;
          illustrated by Anne Catharine Blake.
               p. cm.
     Summary: With the help of smiley-face charts, Josh learns to express his anger appropriately.
          Includes a Note to Parents.
     ISBN 1-59147-000-5 (hardcover : alk. paper) — ISBN 1-59147-001-3 (pbk. : alk. paper)
     1. Anger. [1. Anger. 2. Emotions.]
     I. Blake, Anne Catharine, ill. II. Title.
          BF575.A5D58 2003
          152.4'7—dc21
                                                                          2002154979

Manufactured in the United States of America
10 9 8 7 6 5 4 3 2

Josh's Smiley Faces

A STORY ABOUT
ANGER

written by Gina Ditta-Donahue
illustrated by Anne Catharine Blake

MAGINATION PRESS • WASHINGTON, DC

For Lucas, and all children,
who challenge their parents
to be the best teachers
— GDD

For my dad,
Bud Browning,
the actor
— ACB

Z-o-o-o-o-o-m!
My robot Max saw the aliens
attacking the space troopers.
To the rescue!

Oh no! Max fell apart again.

I got so mad I threw my robot across the room.

Mom said it's not okay to throw things when
I get angry. She took away my space toys.

My baby brother Simon brought me my light saber.
Sometimes I really like playing with Simon.
We have fun together with toys we share.

But if he plays with my train set, I get mad.
Mom told him that the train set is mine, but he tries
to play with it anyway. Last time he played with
my train, I got so mad I hit him with the engine.

Mom said it is not okay
to hurt Simon when I am
mad. She put me on a
time out AND took my
train away.

Mom said it's time for me to start learning how to control my anger. She said that means I need to find something else to do when I'm angry. Throwing and hitting are not okay.

From now on, she said, whenever I get angry I have to use my words and say, "I'm angry" or "I'm mad" or "Help!" Then we can talk about what made me angry or how I need help, so we can fix it.

Mom showed me a big picture with empty circles all over it. She said this was my smiley face chart. Every time I used my words and talked about being mad, I would get a smiley face in one of the circles.

12

Whenever I filled up all the circles on a page
with smiley faces, I could choose a special
treat, like renting a movie, or pizza for supper,
or making a tent in the living room!

But when I threw a toy, the toy would go into the time out box for the rest of the day. I would get the toy back in the morning to try again to play nicely with it.

Mom said if I hit anyone with a toy, then the toy would be put in the time out box AND I would get a time out, too.

Mom said she would put the smiley face chart on
the wall. Then I could see it and remember to use my
words when I get mad. Mom said she would help me
remember, too. She asked what I wanted for my first
special treat. "Pizza for supper!" I said.

Mom said, "That sounds great!"
We drew a picture of a pizza on my
smiley face chart. With pepperoni!
Then we hung it on the wall.

Hey! Simon was playing with my favorite space trooper toy. I grabbed it away and got ready to hit him. Mom said, "Pizza!" I stopped just in time.

I said, "I'm angry!"
Mom said, "What's making you angry?"
"Simon's playing with my toy," I said.

Mom asked me to choose another toy for my brother to play with and to trade with him.

Simon traded toys with me.

"Good job, guys," said Mom.
Then Mom gave me and Simon a kiss…
and me a smiley face!

I got three more smiley faces by using words!

Then I was playing with my take-a-part motorcycle.
I tried to put it together, but the pieces wouldn't fit.
I threw the motorcycle. Argh!

Mom put the pieces in the time out box.
She said, "Remember, use your words.
And remember that you can always ask for help."
She said I could have the toy back in the morning.

I got mad at Mom.
I went to my room
and started to take all
my clothes out of
my dresser.

I dumped them
in the middle of the floor.

Mom came to my door.
"Wow! What a mess," she said.
I told her I was mad.
"Do you know what you're mad about?" she asked.
I said, "Because it's hard to get smiley faces."
She said she would help me, and that I could start
by cleaning up my clothes.

I picked up all the clothes and put them back in
the dresser. Mom helped. She said that learning
to use words when you're mad takes practice.
She said she thinks I'm learning really well.

Then I saw my brother with my baseball mitt.
I picked up his stuffed dog and handed it to him.
"Here, Simon," I said, "here's your toy."

I took my mitt. Simon didn't mind,
and Mom smiled.
"Great idea to make a trade!" she said.
"I'm so proud of you."

She gave me a big hug
and one more smiley face!

My smiley face chart was full!
I said I wanted pepperoni pizza
for supper.

Yippee!

I will keep practicing. I will use my words, and
I can ask for help. When I get really, really good at it,
I wonder if my special treat can be a trip to outer
space to visit my favorite space trooper!

Note to Parents

by Virginia Shiller, Ph.D.

As adults well know, anger is among the most intense of emotions. When faced with frustrations, failures, or perceived slights, anger is a normal human response. In our own lives, as we grew to adulthood, we learned (more or less successfully!) to modulate our expression of anger. However, even though as adults we rarely give physical expression to our anger, we are familiar with the way angry feelings can quickly surface, flood us with powerful and very unpleasant sensations, and on occasion cause us to act in ways or say things we later regret.

The ability to control expressions of anger is largely a learned skill, and parents play a crucial role in teaching children ways to control their anger. This critical job is quite challenging, in part because parents themselves frequently become distressed, embarrassed, or angry in the face of their child's temper outbursts.

When parents respond with punishment or scoldings, they may squelch one particular episode of anger. However, the risk is that children will not learn positive ways of handling this emotion. They may feel only shame, or anger toward the parent for what they see as harsh or unsympathetic behavior. While parents who use only negative approaches may eventually succeed in taming their angry child, it will likely be at the cost of burdening the child with feelings she has no way of expressing. And the child will fail to learn to channel anger into productive patterns of standing up for herself and asserting her needs. The positive side of anger is that it can provide the impetus to persevere in overcoming obstacles and achieving important goals in life.

Josh's Smiley Faces introduces the idea of using a reward plan that provides incentives for children to work on verbalizing their angry feelings, while at the same time providing penalties for physical outbursts. Reward plans that combine positive incentives plus limit-setting penalties are quite useful when children's behavior is potentially hurtful to others.

When you read this book with your child, you can enhance its usefulness in the following ways:

☺ Communicate your understanding of Josh's feelings of frustration when he throws a toy or strikes his brother. "Wow, Josh was having so much fun! It's awfully hard when things you've made fall apart just when you're having a great time!" Helping a child feel understood gives him the emotional support he needs to muster the energy to control his behavior.

☺ Empathize with Josh's unhappiness when his toys are taken away or he is given time out. "It's really hard to have to stop playing when you're having fun. But going to time out does help kids calm down and get ready to play again." Here, you're encouraging your child to see the value of the limits you impose.

☺ Ask your child to think of strategies for Josh to avoid throwing toys. "I wonder how Josh can remember not to throw things when he's mad. Maybe his mom can give him a secret signal when he's starting to get upset? Or maybe he could bring out his favorite bear to sit next to him and remind him to work hard to earn his reward."

☺ If your child's anger is frequently directed at siblings, encourage an open discussion about feelings of jealousy and rivalry, using Josh and his brother Simon as an example. Also, con-

The Smiley Faces Reward Plan

BY GINA DITTA-DONAHUE

The Smiley Faces plan is a simple, easy-to-follow program for children ages 3-6. By following these basic steps and principles, you can help your young child learn to express natural feelings of anger in ways that are healthy and appropriate.

☺ Sit down in a comfortable place with your child. Explain that all people, even grownups, get angry from time to time. Tell him that throwing and hitting are not okay, but there is an okay way to express anger: use your words. Say you're going to help him learn to use words, and reassure him that he'll be able to do it with practice and your help.

☺ Use a very simple chart to keep track of your child's positive behavior. Every instance of appropriate behavior earns her a smiley face (or sticker, etc.). You may copy the chart on the endpaper of this book or make your own. Your child may decorate her chart if she wishes.

☺ Explain that when all the smiley faces are filled in, the child gets a reward. Avoid making the plan too difficult (e.g., too many circles to fill in before earning a reward, too hard to earn each smiley face)

or too complicated (e.g., a confusing hierarchy of rewards).

☺ Offer a short list of rewards from which the child may choose. It is perfectly fine if he changes his mind and wants a different reward from the list at any time. Be completely flexible and enthusiastic. The point is to empower your child's ability to make choices and control the outcome of his behavior.

☺ Display the chart where it will be in view as much as possible throughout the day.

☺ Watch closely for small opportunities to reward your child with a smiley face, especially in the beginning. Then she will get the idea and learn to work for the reward. Encourage her and remind her of the treat she is working toward.

☺ Celebrate your child's success in ways he enjoys each time he earns a smiley face: a hug and kiss, a high-five, "I'm so proud of you" and other praise.

☺ Review all the smiley faces on her chart at the end of the day and what she did to earn each one. This repetition will help reinforce desirable behavior.

☺ Always give the chosen reward as

soon as possible once the chart has been completed.

☺ Spell out simple penalties for inappropriate behaviors in advance. If the child throws a toy, the toy goes into a time out box for the rest of the day and will be returned the next morning. A time out box should be large enough to accommodate several toys at a time. Keep it out of general view (your room is a good place), and don't decorate it or make a big deal out of it.

☺ If the child hurts another person or a pet, the child gets a time out himself. The time out period should be appropriate for his age and temperament. A good starting rule of thumb is one minute of time out for each year of age (e.g., 5 minutes for a 5-year-old).

☺ Never take a smiley face away once it has been awarded.

☺ When your child is angry, help her find the words to express the anger, especially at first. Have her repeat after you: "I'm mad! My toy won't work! Help!" or "I'm angry! He is playing with my train."

☺ Continue using new smiley face charts until your child's behavior is reliable.

sider your own behavior and be sure that the time required to care for a baby or toddler has not resulted in depriving your older child of needed attention. Comments such as, "I'll bet it's hard for you when I have to spend so much time feeding and taking care of your brother" help your older child feel understood and less alone with his feelings.

In designing and carrying out a reward plan with your child, keep the following in mind:

☺ Introduce the plan in a positive manner. You can express confidence in how she has mastered other things, such as learning to ride her bike, and that you believe she is "grown up enough" to work on using her words when she is angry.

☺ Make the reward attainable within a time frame that's appropriate for your child's age and temperament. Parents usually have a good sense as to whether their child can wait an hour, a day, or a week to earn a reward. Obviously, if rewards must be available frequently, they must be kept modest!

☺ While at times the offer of a new toy may be appropriate as a reward, try to think of non-materialistic alternatives. Special activities or special time with a parent can be very enticing to a child.

☺ Give your child support and reminders to help him achieve the goal. In this story, Mom calls out "Pizza!" just as Josh is ready to hit Simon. This kind of reminder both assures your child that you're rooting for his success and it contributes to the learning process.

☺ If your child is having difficulty achieving success, you can shape her behavior by being generous in interpreting minor behaviors as worthy of rewards. If your child frowns, looks angry, but doesn't immediately hit her friend, you could offer a smiley face and compliment your child on her self-control. By offering the smiley face, you're leading your child in the right direction, and increasing her confidence that if she tries hard she can do it.

☺ When you must give penalties such as time out, avoid expressing anger at your child for the misbehavior. "Oops, you made a mistake. I'm afraid you're going to have to go to time out for 5 minutes." By administering a penalty in a sympathetic manner, you encourage your child to regret his own actions rather than to focus his anger on you for being mean.

☺ Consider how siblings will react to one child having a reward plan. In this story, Josh's little brother Simon might want to get smiley faces like his older brother does, but he wouldn't understand the connection between the smiley faces and the larger reward. Josh's mother could explain to Josh that she will give Simon smiley faces so that he won't feel left out, but that he won't get to pick his own special rewards.

☺ The reward plan will work best if all adults in the child's daily life are aware and supportive of the plan.

It takes time and energy on your part to put together and carry out a reward plan. You might want to wait for a time when you have the emotional energy and available time to carry through with it. But in the end, both your child and you should feel well rewarded. You've worked together to reach an important goal. For your child, invisible rewards such as greater acceptance by peers and less negative attention from adults will kick in to reinforce success. And it always feels good as a parent to solve a problem in a constructive and creative way!

Virginia Shiller, Ph.D., is a clinical psychologist in private practice in New Haven, Connecticut, and a Lecturer at the Yale Child Study Center. She is the author, with Meg Schneider, of Rewards for Kids! Ready-to-Use Charts and Reward Activities for Positive Parenting.

About the Author

GINA DITTA-DONAHUE is a psychiatric registered nurse. The inspiration for *Josh's Smiley Faces,* her first children's book, came from the patients with whom she has worked, as well as her own toddler. She lives in Southern California with her husband and two sons.

About the Illustrator

ANNE CATHARINE BLAKE is a writer, graphic designer, cartoonist, and illustrator, with many children's books to her credit. She grew up in Canada and the southern United States, and currently lives in Portland, Oregon.